Name _____

Read this story. Write the words from "Grizzle's Grumble" in the sentences. Read the story again with your words.

began	giants	louder
bigger	grumbled	problem
cookie	heard	sadder

Little Dab was very small for his age. Every morning he tried to make his voice sound

_____. Every night he tried to make his

chest look _____. But every day he just grew

_____.

"It's no use," he said. "I am small, small, small!"

A little boy _____ Little Dab. "What is your

_____?" he asked.

"I want to be big and loud like the _____ I

have read about," Little Dab _____. He

_____ to cry.

"But I would be afraid of someone as big as a giant," said the little boy. "A little friend would be just right for

me. Would you like to share this _____ with me?"

 Write sentences to tell about something that makes you grumble.

© D.C. Heath and Company

"Grizzle's Grumble," pages 10–15
Vocabulary: key words

1

In "Grizzle's Grumble," some things cause other things to happen. Read the sentence beginning. Underline the ending that tells what happened.

1. Stout says it's no fun being big because
   his head bumps the trees.
   his hand gets stuck in the cookie jar.

2. Grizzle doesn't like being big because
   nothing fits right.
   nothing sounds right.

3. Grab doesn't like being big because
   he gets socks that shrank in the wash.
   he gets socks with stretched out elastic.

4. Grub doesn't like being big because
   he gets sweaters that are too big.
   he gets sweaters that are stretched out.

5. Dab is so little that
   he can't reach a high shelf.
   his sweater is too big.

6. Grizzle is just the right size, so
   he can take care of big problems.
   he can take care of little problems.

 Think about other big problems that Grizzle could help Dab with. Draw a picture of one. Write a sentence about the problem.

Name _____

Read these sentences about David and his problem. Circle the word that belongs in each sentence. Read the sentence again with your word.

1. David's lunch box was up high in his _____.

   cross   closet   clothes

2. He _____ to reach it, but he was too short.

   stretched   blocked   dragged

3. David began to grumble, and he felt very _____.

   fresh   grouchy   flashy

4. He thought it would be _____ to ask a giant to help him.

   single   smart   sport

5. David's brother Sam came and used a _____ to reach the lunch box.

   glass   stool   plate

6. Sam then _____ carefully off the stool.

   tripped   pranced   stepped

7. David was _____ to have such a helpful brother.

   proud   scared   sly

8. David did not need a giant to _____ a hand after all.

   twist   grasp   lend

 Make a list of the words on this page that begin with the letters cl, str, gr, sm, st, pr, and end with nd. How many words fit under each heading?

"Grizzle's Grumble," pages 10–15
Decoding: initial and final consonant blends

You can change the meaning of a word by changing the ending. Write the root word with es or ed. Remember to change y to i before adding the ending. The first one is done for you.

	Root Word	Drop y, add es	Drop y, add ed
1.	try	tries	tried
2.	carry		
3.	hurry		
4.	bury		
5.	dry		
6.	marry		
7.	family		
8.	city		
9.	pony		
10.	berry		
11.	country		
12.	body		

 Choose three words from any part of the page. Write sentences using the words.

_____

4

"Grizzle Grumble," pages 10–15
Decoding: spelling changes (y to i before ending)

Antonyms are words with opposite meanings.
Read the word in bold print and the sentence.
Circle the antonym for the word in bold print.

1. **spoke**   Stout listened to Grizzle tell why he didn't like
being big.

2. **loud**   No one heard Grizzle's soft grumbling.

3. **few**   There were many books,
but Dab wanted just one.

4. **stupid**   Grab and Grub were smart
to try to reach Dab's book.

5. **frown**   Dab had a big smile on his
face as Grizzle handed him
the book.

6. **yourself**   "Thank you," said Dab. "I
hope I can reach that high
myself someday."

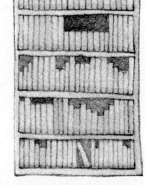

7. **asked**   "You will, I'm sure," answered Grab.

8. **old**   "You are still young. You will grow a lot
more as you get older," said Grub.

Write the words **always, save,** and **before** on
cards. Write the antonym for each word on
the back of the card. Ask a classmate to make up a
sentence for each word and its antonym.

Name _____

Think about how you are like or different from other people and things. Write these sentences to tell about yourself.

1. I am smaller than _____

   _____

   I am as big as _____

   _____

2. I am faster than _____

   _____

   Sometimes I am as slow as _____

   _____

3. When I am sad, I am sadder than _____

   _____

   When I am happy, I am as happy as a _____

   _____

4. I am older than _____

   _____

 Tell how you are like a puffy cloud, a bouncing ball, and a hot potato. Then tell how you are different.

© D.C. Heath and Company

Name _____

Read this story. Write the words from "The Turnip" in the sentences. Read the story again to check your words.

beautiful   Rooster   turnips
Once   together   until

Not long ago, there was a Grandmother Hen who

helped everyone. She helped Grandfather _____
plant the seeds by the house. She helped Mother Hen feed
the baby chicks in the yard. She helped her grandson feed

the pigs behind the barn. _____ she even helped
a neighbor sell corn out by the road. She worked from

morning _____ night.
    Sometimes when the work was done, she felt old and
tired. One night, Grandmother wiped her brow. She said to

Grandfather, "Working _____ in the garden is
fun. But look at my hands. They are as brown as the

_____ that grow in the garden."
    Grandfather took her hand in his. "You do not look old

to me," he said. "To me you are more _____
than any other animal I have ever seen." Grandmother Hen
smiled. Maybe helping others and being tired was not such
a bad thing after all.

 Read the story again and underline all
the things Grandmother Hen did to help others.

Name _____

Think about the order of things that happened in "The Turnip." Read the sentences in each set. Check (✓) the sentence that tells what happened <u>before</u> the numbered sentence.

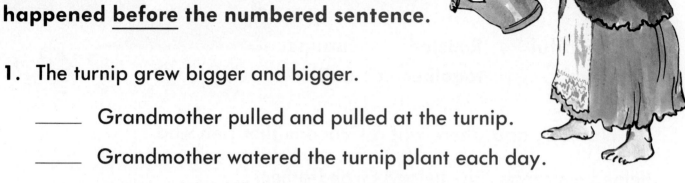

1. The turnip grew bigger and bigger.

    _____ Grandmother pulled and pulled at the turnip.

    _____ Grandmother watered the turnip plant each day.

2. Grandmother hurried to the garden.

    _____ Grandmother woke up early in the morning.

    _____ Grandmother called Micky to help pull.

3. Grandfather asked Grandmother to help pull the turnip.

    _____ The turnip did not move.

    _____ Grandfather shouted for the rooster and the hen.

4. The pig took a very big breath.

    _____ Everyone yelled to the pig to help pull.

    _____ The bird pulled at the pig's tail.

5. All the helpers fell down.

    _____ The bird flew away to his tall tree.

    _____ Suddenly the turnip came out of the ground.

 Read the sentences again. Write a sentence that tells what happened <u>after</u> the numbered sentence.

_____

© D.C. Heath and Company

"Big/Little" and "The Turnip," pages 16–27
Selection Comprehension: sequence

Name _____

Read the sentence and the root word in bold print. Change the root word by adding _er_ or _est_. Write the new word in the sentence. Read the sentence again to check your word.

1. tall   Grandfather was _____ than Micky, but he asked Micky to help pull the turnip.

2. big   The turnip was the _____ that Grandfather had ever seen.

3. short   "How can I help you?" Micky asked Grandfather.

"I am _____ than you."

4. long   "Our chain is too short," said Grandfather.

"We need a _____ one."

5. fast   Micky and the dog ran to the tool shed,

but Micky ran _____ .

6. hard   Of all the people pulling, Grandfather

pulled the _____ .

7. loud   The noise coming up from the ground was the

_____ noise Grandfather had ever heard.

8. small   "Next time I will grow a _____ turnip than this one," said Grandfather.

 Write four sentences using words with _er_ and _est_.

_____

Some words with two parts begin with a and be. Read the sentence and the words in bold print. Circle the word that belongs in the sentence. Read the sentence with your word.

1. Nicky fell _____ in the hay, but he came running when Grandmother called.
   awake   asleep   alike

2. Nicky sat _____ Grandmother, mixing the cookie dough.
   beneath   beside   behave

3. Then they put the dough _____ them on the table and rolled it out flat.
   belong   beyond   between

4. After baking, the dough _____ very good cookies.
   became   betrayed   belonged

5. Grandmother told Nicky to line up the cookies _____ the windowsill to cool.
   away   along   alike

6. When people _____ to help each other, things get done.
   alarm   against   agree

 Write all the a and be words in two rows. Write each word in parts. Share your list with the class. Add other words.

© D.C. Heath and Company

"Big/Little" and "The Turnip," pages 16–27
Decoding: word parts a-, be-

Name _____

Read this story about two princesses. Write what is the same and what is different in the boxes.

There was once a princess who lived in the city. Her cousin lived in the country. She was a princess too. The city princess lived in a tall brown house. The country princess lived in a small white house on a farm. But they both liked music. The city princess liked to go out at night to hear beautiful band music. The country princess liked the morning music of the birds.

Both Girls
lived in _____
liked _____

City Princess	Country Princess

 Think of more ways the princesses could be alike and different. Write your ideas.

The author of "The Turnip" described or told about something really big. Think of something that you can describe. Answer these questions to help you describe it.

What I will write about _____

_____

How does it look? (size, color, shape) _____

_____

How does it sound? _____

_____

How does it feel? _____

_____

How does it taste or smell? _____

_____

Other ideas _____

_____

_____

Share your writing plan in class. Add other ideas. On other paper, write what you have described on the plan. Then put the writing in your folder.

_____

"Big/Little" and "The Turnip," pages 16–27
Language: writing process (prewriting)

Name _____

Think about how these words from "What's So Big About That?" can be put together. Read the headings and write the words that belong together.

around	facts	largest	tallest
biggest	George	pumpkin	telephone poles
Chester Zoo	heaviest	Saint Bernard	Washington
England	helicopter	second graders	

People or Animals

_____

_____

_____

Places

_____

_____

_____

Things or Ideas

_____

_____

_____

Size

_____

_____

_____

Other

_____

 Choose a word from each list to write a sentence. Share your sentence with classmates.

Name _____

Complete this chart with facts from "What's So Big About That?" Use your book to help you. Then answer the questions.

What	World Record	Size
George, the giraffe	_____	_____
Saint Bernard	_____	_____
redwood	_____	_____
pumpkin	_____	_____
pancake	_____	_____

1. What weighed more—the pumpkin or the pancake?

   _____ How much did it weigh? _____

2. What weighed more—the Saint Bernard or the pumpkin?

   _____ How much did it weigh? _____

3. What world record does the redwood hold?

   _____

4. What world record does the giraffe hold?

   _____

 Think of one thing that could set a world record. Describe it. Then share it with your class in a "Class Book of World Records."

The letters _ph_ stand for the beginning sound in _phone_. Read the sentence and the words in bold print. Circle the word that belongs in the sentence. Read the sentence with your word.

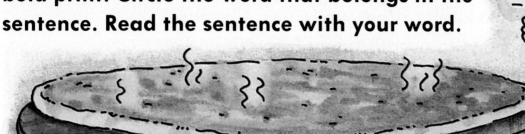

1. I would like to take a picture of the largest pancake. Then I could show the _____ to all my friends.

   telephone   photo   elephant

2. What would I do if I saw the biggest pumpkin? I'd call my sister on the _____ and tell her to hurry over.

   graph   phase   telephone

3. The fastest train in the world is in France. A _____ shows it goes much faster than other trains.

   phantom   graph   phase

4. I can talk very fast. I'll bet that I can say the _____ faster than you can.

   alphabet   pheasant   photograph

5. I had a dream last night about many famous people. I got more _____ than anyone else did.

   telephones   phrases   autographs

 Find other words in your book with the letters _ph_ that stand for the beginning consonant sound in **phone**. Make a list of the words.

Name _____

Read these sentences about different kinds of trees. Then answer the questions.

There are two kinds of redwood trees. One kind is very tall. It grows to over 300 feet high. The other kind is very wide. The largest tree is 103 feet around.

1. What do these sentences tell about? _____

2. What is the most important idea in these sentences?

    _____

3. What facts tell about this idea?

    a. _____

    b. _____

A redwood forest is a dark place. The giant trees grow close together. They shut out most of the sunlight. There are very few plants on the forest floor.

4. What is the most important idea in these sentences?

    _____

5. What facts tell about this idea?

    a. _____

    b. _____

 How many children would it take to make a circle 103 feet around a redwood tree?

"What's So Big About That?" pages 28–31
Comprehension: topic/main idea/details

Read these facts about a record for the Guinness book. Write the description.

The Guinness Record　The largest pumpkin in the world weighed 703 pounds.

Who　Mr. Dean Jones

Where and When　He grew the pumpkin in his backyard during the summer of 2000.

How and Why　Mr. Jones watered and fed the pumpkin plant food every day. He wanted to have the biggest jack-o'-lantern in the world.

Mr. Jones' Record in the *Guinness Book of World Records*

_____

_____

_____

_____

_____

_____

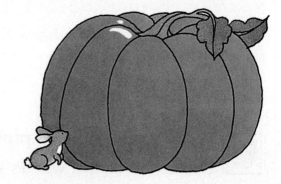

Share your writing in class. Then plan and write your own record for the Guinness book. Put the writing in your folder.

Name _____

Some of the words on this page are in "What Makes a Shadow?" Read the sentence and the meaning. Write the word from the sentence that matches the meaning.

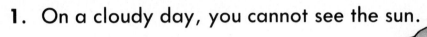

1. On a cloudy day, you cannot see the sun.

   a lot of clouds _____

2. If you turn on the light, the darkness goes away.

   no light _____

3. Earth is a long way from the sun,
   but the sun's heat can still warm you.

   the planet you live on _____

4. On a hot day, you can play in the shade of a big tree.

   a place where the sun's light is blocked _____

5. The sun shines on you in the day, and other stars shine on you at night.

   gives light _____

6. When you stand in the sunlight, you can make a shadow.

   a dark place where the sun's light is blocked

   _____

 Write about how to play Tag with shadows.
Use some of the words you wrote on this page.

© D.C. Heath and Company

"What Makes a Shadow?" pages 34–37
Vocabulary: key words

Name _____

This page tells about "What Makes a Shadow?" Read the sentences that tell what happens. Write sentences to tell why. Use your book. Write the page numbers for the answers.

1. You can see your shadow behind you. Why? _____

_____ page _____

2. Your shadow moves. Why? _____

_____ page _____

3. You can never catch your shadow. Why? _____

_____ page _____

4. There is a shadow on one side of the house. Why? _____

_____

_____ page _____

5. It is a cloudy day. Why? _____

_____ page _____

6. The shadow makes the night. Why? _____

_____ page _____

 Draw a sunny day picture and a cloudy day picture. Write sentences that tell what happened and why in the pictures.

**These riddles can be solved with words that end
with <u>dge</u> as in <u>badge</u>. Write the word that solves
the riddle.**

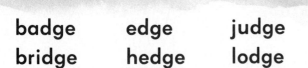

badge   edge   judge
bridge   hedge   lodge

1. I help choose the winners in a contest.

   What am I? _____

2. I am a row of bushes in your yard.

   What am I? _____

3. I am a small cabin in the woods or near a lake.

   What am I? _____

4. I help people and cars get across rivers or streams.

   What am I? _____

5. I am shiny. A police officer wears me.

   What am I? _____

6. I am the rim or side of something.

   What am I? _____

 Say the meaning of a word in bold print. Ask
a classmate to name the word.

Name _____

Each sentence has a silly word. Read the sentence. Use the clues to choose a real word for the sentence. Circle the word. Read the sentence with the real word.

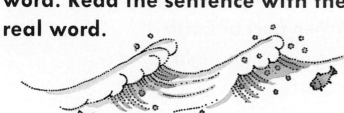

1. It is very warm in the <u>hinkle</u>. In <u>hinkle</u>, you can splash in the waves. What is <u>hinkle</u>?

      weather   shadow   summer

2. On a cloudy day, you might need an <u>iggish</u>. My dad carries an <u>iggish</u> to work when it rains. What is <u>iggish</u>?

      umbrella   animal   eggshell

3. On a clear night, you might see the <u>stodge</u> in the sky. Sometimes there is a full <u>stodge</u>; sometimes there is a half <u>stodge</u>. What is <u>stodge</u>?

      stars   owl   moon

4. We planted flowers on the <u>clem</u> side of our house. There is too much shade in the north, but the <u>clem</u> side is very sunny. What is <u>clem</u>?

      sun   south   porch

 Write a sentence using a silly word. Give clues for the real word that belongs in the sentence. Ask a classmate to guess the real word.

Read these sentences. Think about the important ideas. Check (✓) the answers.

Night and day come and go. Earth keeps turning in space. The sun keeps shining. When part of Earth faces the sun, it is day. At the same time, it is night on the other side of Earth. Children are sleeping and dreaming.

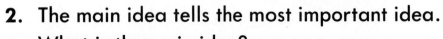

1. The topic tells what the sentences are about. What is the topic?

    _____ stars

    _____ night and day

2. The main idea tells the most important idea. What is the main idea?

    _____ Night and day come and go.

    _____ Earth faces the sun.

3. The details tell about the main idea. What are the details?

    _____ Day changes to night because Earth is turning in space.

    _____ Children are sleeping and dreaming.

    _____ Earth keeps turning in space.

 Make a list of things that are the same and different about night and day.

"What Makes a Shadow?" pages 34–37
Comprehension: topic/main idea/details

As you read each story, think about what could happen next. Underline the answer. Then tell why you think so.

1. Elena hid her eyes. "One, two, three," she began. The other children ran away quickly. Elena called out, "Ready or not, here I come!"

   What will probably happen next?
   Elena will sit down and start to count.
   Elena will try to find the other children.

   Why do you think it will happen?

   _____

   _____

2. Mr. Luke walked down the sidewalk. It had been a nice morning, but now a cold wind began to blow. Dark clouds covered the sun.

   What will probably happen next?
   The sun will set.
   Rain will begin to fall.

   Why do you think it will happen?

   _____

   _____

 Choose one of the stories on this page and write a different ending.

_____

Name _____

**Read this story. Write the words from
"Bear Shadow" in the sentences. Read
the story again to check your words.**

field	hammer	open
follow	higher	shovel

Rabbit found a trail in the _____ of tall

grass. She started to _____ the trail. Up and up

it went. As Rabbit climbed _____ , she thought
she heard a noise. "It sounds like someone is pounding nails

with a _____ ," she thought.

Just then, Rabbit saw Bear _____ his shed

door a crack. She watched Bear take out a _____
and begin to dig a hole. Suddenly Bear stopped and said,
"Rabbit, is that your shadow I see near my house?"

 Write a sentence that tells Rabbit's answer to
Bear's question.

"Bear Shadow," pages 38–45
Vocabulary: key words

© D.C. Heath and Company

Name _____

This page tells what happened in "Bear Shadow."
Read the sentence and question. Check (✓) the
sentence that tells why.

1. Bear hid behind a tree.
   Why didn't he see his shadow?

   _____ He ran away from it.

   _____ The shade of the tree hid the shadow.

2. Bear was at the top of a cliff.
   Why was he upset?

   _____ He could not get down.

   _____ He could not get rid of his shadow.

3. It was almost noon and Bear's shadow was gone.
   Why was the shadow gone?

   _____ The sun was high in the sky.

   _____ Bear put the shadow in a hole and left it there.

4. Later, Bear caught a fish.
   Why did he catch a fish when he tried again?

   _____ His shadow fell on a different part of the pond.

   _____ The shadow was still back at Bear's house.

 Did Bear and his shadow become friends at the
end of the story? Tell what you think and why.

Read this story. Many words have the vowel sounds in <u>lie</u> and <u>chief</u>. Underline the words. Then write the words under <u>lie</u> and <u>chief</u>.

Bear was very happy with the berry pie she had just made. She couldn't wait to have a piece. Bear could tell by the shadows that it was still afternoon. She had spied some nice fish in the pond. She would fish before dinner.

Bear went through the field to get to the pond. She tried to catch some fish, but she was not lucky. She fell asleep as the sun dried her fur. After a brief nap, she went back to the woods to have berry pie. But when she got there, the other bears told her a thief had taken the pie. Bear couldn't believe it! She looked at the other bears. She knew they were telling a lie. They had the pie all over their faces!

lie   chief

_____   _____

_____   _____

_____   _____

_____   _____

_____   _____

 Find words in your book that have the vowel sounds in **lie** and **chief**. Put the words in lists under **lie** and **chief**. Add your own words.

As you read each story, think about what will happen. Put a check (✓) beside the sentence that tells what will probably happen next.

1. Jill's mother said she could make some popcorn. She put the popcorn in the pan, but she forgot to put the lid on. Then she held the pan over the fire. What will probably happen next?

_____ Popcorn will pop out of the pan.

_____ Jill will share the popcorn with her family.

2. Lee and Meg saw many ducks swimming in the pond. "Did you bring anything to feed the ducks?" asked Meg. Mrs. George gave bread to the children. What will probably happen next?

_____ Mrs. George will say it is time to go home.

_____ The children will feed the ducks.

3. "May I go out and play with Kevin and Mark?" Phil asked his mother.
    "You may play with them after you put on something warm," she said. "It's very cold and windy."
    What will probably happen next?

_____ Phil will put on his warm coat.

_____ Phil's friends will go home.

 Choose one of the stories from this page. Write a different ending for it.

Name _____

Help Bear put his things in ABC order. Read each list of Bear's things. Write each list in ABC order.

1. Bear's closet:

   socks _____

   slacks _____

   shirts _____

   skates _____

2. Bear's toys:

   blocks _____

   bell _____

   boat _____

   ball _____

3. Bear's food:

   fish _____

   fowl _____

   flies _____

   frogs _____

4. Bear's friends:

   Mort _____

   Mike _____

   Mark _____

   Meg _____

 What are your favorite playthings? Write the names of four things in ABC order.

Read the words from "Science Fun." Write the words in the sentences. Read the sentences to check your words.

chalk   create   somebody   wiggle

circles   fuzzy   thicker

1. You can make or _____ a sidewalk shadow drawing.

2. You may want a friend

   or _____ to help you.

3. Use _____ to make the drawing.

4. Draw lines and _____ .

5. Make fatter lines with

   _____ chalk.

6. Don't _____ your hand as you draw.

7. You could get a funny, _____ picture!

 Make a sidewalk shadow drawing.
Write a What Am I riddle.

Name _____

Think about what happened in "Science Fun."
Check (✓) the sentence that tells a fact
that belongs with the numbered sentence.

1. The morning sun is low, and sunlight is slanted.

   _____ The shadows are long.

   _____ The shadows are fuzzy.

2. The sun moves higher in the sky.

   _____ The shadows grow shorter.

   _____ The shadows grow darker.

3. A thin cloud covers the sun.

   _____ The shadows get brighter.

   _____ The shadows are fuzzy.

4. You put your hand in front of the flashlight.

   _____ A dark hand shape is in the circle of light.

   _____ A dark circle is in the circle of light.

5. Wax paper covers the light from the flashlight.

   _____ The shadows look fuzzy.

   _____ The shadows grow longer.

 Write directions with four steps for a friend to make an animal shadow on a wall.

Some words have two parts or syllables. Read the sentence. Underline the word with two parts. Then write the two parts of the word.

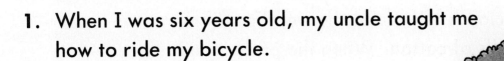

1. When I was six years old, my uncle taught me how to ride my bicycle.

_____

2. I didn't think I would be able to do it.

_____

3. The handle bars seemed too big to hold.

_____

4. They would wobble and shake if I tried to go too fast.

_____

5. One day, I took a tumble.

_____

6. I hurt my ankle.

_____

7. But now I have no trouble at all riding my bike.

_____

 Write these words on cards: sniffle, people, tickle, maple, waddle, puzzle. Ask a classmate to tell the two parts of each word.

© D.C. Heath and Company

Name _____

**Read these sentences. Think about the
important ideas. Check (✓) the answers.**

Weather reporters use clouds to tell about the weather.
The shapes of the clouds tell about the weather. Some
clouds look like balls of cotton. When the puffy clouds
become dark and heavy with water, they cause storms.
Another kind of cloud looks like flat, gray sheets. If these
clouds touch the ground, they are called ground fog.

1. The topic tells what the sentences are about.
   What is the topic?

   _____ storms

   _____ clouds

2. The main idea tells the most important idea.
   What is the main idea?

   _____ Reporters use clouds to tell about the weather.

   _____ Water in some clouds forms pieces of ice.

3. The details tell about the main idea.
   What are the details?

   _____ Puffy clouds can cause storms.

   _____ Flat gray clouds can become ground fog.

   _____ Clouds look like feathers.

 Add one fact about clouds to this page.

Read each list of words. Circle the list that is in ABC order. Use the alphabet to help you.

a b c d e f g h i j k
l m
n o
p q
r s t
u v
w x
y z

1. dark   hurry   shape   turnip
   deal   hole   slant   throw
   duck   hit   sock   tear
   dog   haste   sunk   tall

2. rope   sang   pride   heavy
   ran   shade   puff   hand
   red   song   pound   hot
   right   stuck   planted   huff

3. tell   nail   blue   crate
   try   near   beast   catch
   tail   noon   bone   chair
   thick   nut   band   cloud

4. bird   fine   mate   wash
   barn   frost   might   weld
   beach   face   mold   work
   boil   fur   mess   write

 Write the names of five people you know. Then put the names in ABC order.

Name _____

Read this story. Write the words from "Drakestail" in the sentences. Read the story again to check your words.

chicken   frightened   pocket   servants

fifty   money   scenes   towards

Drakestail does not like everything about castle life. He does not like castle animals, but the one he likes least of

all is the _____ . He is _____ by the buzzing wasps that fly around the castle yard. When the

sheep run _____ Drakestail, he runs into the castle. Drakestail has fifty gold coins, so he thinks he has

a lot of _____ . He keeps his money in his jacket

_____ . Drakestail is one of _____ helpers who work for the king. These helpers who work in the

castle are called _____ . The king and Drakestail

like to watch funny plays. The _____ make everyone laugh.

Write these words on your paper: hen, scared, coins. Look at this page and find a synonym for each word. Write the word next to its synonym.

Name _____

Think about the order of things that happened in "Drakestail." Read each sentence. Draw a line to the sentence that tells what happened next. Connect the dots to make the lines.

What Happened?	What Happened Next?
1. Drakestail counted his money. •	• Ladder made himself very small.
2. Drakestail gave the king some money. •	• The king asked if he could have some money.
3. Drakestail said Ladder could see the king with him. •	• Drakestail was put in with the chickens.
4. Drakestail got to the king's gate. •	• The king said he would pay Drakestail back.

5. Drakestail was put into the well. •	• River hurried to help Drakestail.
6. Drakestail was put into a fire. •	• Ladder helped Drakestail.
7. The wasps flew out of Drakestail's pocket. •	• The king ran away.

 Drakestail rested on the king's throne. What happened next? Write your answer.

Name _____

Read these sentences about Drakestail.
Choose the word with <u>er</u> or <u>est</u> for each sentence.
Write the word in the sentence. Read the
sentence to check your word.

1. The king was the _____ man in the story.
   meaner   meanest

2. Drakestail was the _____ duck in the land.
   nicer   nicest

3. Ladder made himself _____ and jumped into
   Drakestail's pocket.
   smaller   smallest

4. Fox, River, and Ladder made Drakestail's pocket the

   _____ one in town!
   heavier   heaviest

5. Drakestail was _____ than the king.
   smarter   smartest

6. Drakestail was the _____ one in the story.
   braver   bravest

7. Drakestail had always been _____ than the king.
   happier   happiest

 For each answer, write the root word.

"Drakestail," pages 52–67
Decoding: comparative/superlative -er, -est

You can change a word to mean more than one by changing the ending. Write each root word with the new ending es. First change f to v.

Root Word	Change f to v and add es
wolf	_____
leaf	_____
life	_____
shelf	_____
half	_____
knife	_____

Write the words in the letter.

Dear Ken,

Yesterday I helped Mom and Dad rake _____ .

Then we cleaned the tool _____ in the garage. Dad

found two old, but good cutting _____ so we cut

apples into _____ and ate them. Later, walking on

a trail, we saw some _____ . Our _____

have been very different since we moved here!

Your friend,

Bill

 Write sentences using the words elf, calf, and
scarf to mean more than one.

Name _____

Read this story about Drakestail.
Think about what happens.
Answer the questions.

    King Drakestail lived in the beautiful country of Bright Woods. He helped his people and they helped him.

    One day, the people came to Drakestail. "The Wasps of Dark Woods want to fight with us," they said.

    "Ask them to come and see how happy our people are," said the king.

    When the Wasps of Dark Woods came to Bright Woods, they asked, "Will you teach us how to be happy?"

    " Yes, we will," said Drakestail.

1. What kind of king was Drakestail? _____

_____

2. Where did Drakestail live? _____

_____

3. What did the Wasps of Dark Woods want? _____

_____

4. How did Drakestail stop the Wasps from fighting?

_____

_____

 What happens at the end of the story?
Write your answer.

"Drakestail," pages 52–67
Comprehension: character traits/goals/setting/plot

© D.C. Heath and Company

When you read, look for clues to what will happen next. Read each part of the story and the questions. Check (✓) the sentence that tells what will probably happen next.

Drakestail's sister Ducky came to visit. "I haven't seen you in a long time," she said sadly.

1. What will Ducky probably say next?

_____ "Would you like to move away?"

_____ "I am so glad to see you."

The people met Ducky and danced all night. Ducky said, "The land where I live is not much fun."

2. What will Drakestail probably say next?

_____ "Let's move there."

_____ "I think you should move here."

Ducky was very happy. "I would love to live in your land," she said. "The people are very nice."

3. What will Ducky probably do?

_____ Ducky will hurry home to pack.

_____ Ducky will walk home sadly.

 Read the story again and discuss the clues that helped you decide your answers.

© D.C. Heath and Company

"Drakestail," pages 52–67
Comprehension: predict outcomes

Read the story. Write the words from "The Cats' Burglar" in the sentences. Read the story again to check your words. Then write each word with its meaning.

burglar   police   should

chief   quiet

Last night, someone took the clock from my sister's

bedroom. We called the _____ station. Soon

the _____ came in his blue car to help us.

The police chief told us that a _____
must have taken the clock. The burglar had been very

_____. We were lucky that he did not steal

anything else. The chief told us that we _____
put better locks on our doors and windows.

1. the top person in charge _____

2. people who make sure laws are obeyed _____

3. ought to _____

4. not making a noise _____

5. a person who steals things _____

Write three sentences about police jobs.

_____

**Each P sentence tells about a
problem in "The Cats' Burglar."
Next to S, tell how the problem
was solved. Write the page
numbers for the answers.**

1. P People laughed at Aunt Emma because she had many cats.

   S Aunt Emma _____

   _____ page _____

2. P The cats had to let Aunt Emma know that something
      was wrong.

   S The cats _____

   _____ page _____

3. P A stranger was in Aunt Emma's house.

   S Aunt Emma _____

   _____ page _____

4. P Scruffy wanted the feather on the burglar's hat.

   S Scruffy _____

   _____ page _____

 How did the burglar solve his sneezing problem?

_____

What a person says often tells something about that person. Read what people said in "The Cats' Burglar." Then write what it tells about that person.

Who said this?	What does it tell about the person?
1. "Isn't he cute?" said _____	_____
2. "Look at them. They are ripping up everything," said _____	_____
3. "Burglar or not, I must find Baby Bear," said _____	_____
4. "Achoo! I can't—achoo—move!" said _____	_____

 Write other words or sentences that tell what Aunt Emma is like.

_____

"Cats" and "The Cats' Burglar," pages 70–81
Comprehension: character traits

Name _____

Read this story about a cat with a problem.
Write how the problem was solved.

Shadow was a dark gray cat. She liked to play tricks on the family she lived with. At bedtime, she would hide. When people came by, she would jump out and frighten them.

One day the family came home with a new cat. "She is so clean and pretty," they said. "Let's name her Snow White."

Shadow did not like Snow White. One rainy day, she hid in the leaves outside. Snow White came by. Shadow jumped out at her. Snow White jumped high in the air. She landed in the mud. Now Snow White looked very much like Shadow.

1. What was Shadow's problem?

   _____

2. What did Shadow do about her problem?

   _____

3. What else might Shadow have done to solve her problem?

   _____

   _____

   _____

   _____

 If you owned Shadow and Snow White, what would you do to solve this problem? Write your answer.

   _____

You need nonfiction books (books with facts) to write a report about cats. Read the book titles on the shelf. Write the titles of the books that will help you with your report.

_____

_____

_____

_____

_____

_____

Choose one of the nonfiction cat books. Draw a cover for it. Write the title on the cover. Write sentences that tell what you think the book is about.

"Cats" and "The Cats' Burglar," pages 70–81
Study Skills: reference sources (library)

This story about a pet cat needs some ideas to make it more interesting. Choose ideas from the box or add your own. Write the story.

> • thick, orange fur
> • bushy tail
> • always hungry
> • eats three cans of cat food
> • jumps on the kitchen table
> • licks the plates clean

My friend Lucy has a pet cat. Lucy calls the cat Hungry. Every day, Hungry eats cat food and anything else she can find.

_____

_____

_____

_____

_____

_____

Share your writing in class. Then take the writing from your folder and add details to make it more interesting. Put the writing in your folder.

Name _____

Read these sentences and the words from "Cat Habits." Circle all the words that make sense in each sentence. Then read each sentence with the words you circled.

1. Most cats do what they like to do. My cat has some funny _____ .

    habits
    spots
    manners

2. Sometimes he sleeps in a chair. Other times he sleeps on my _____ .

    pillow
    belly
    branch

3. He gets silly. He likes to chase his _____ toy.

    special
    only
    favorite

4. My cat shows his feelings. He arches his back when he is _____ .

    afraid
    turning
    angry

5. _____ , when he feels happy, he climbs up on the lamp shade and sleeps.

    Since
    Later
    Afterward

 Habits can be good or bad. Write about a good habit. Then write about a bad habit. Tell how to change it.

"Why Cat Eats First and Washes Afterward" and "Cat Habits," pages 82–88
Vocabulary: key words

In "Cat Habits," you read about cats and their habits. Read the headings and fill in the missing facts.

Cat Habits

How a cat talks

_____

_____

_____

_____

How a cat plays

_____

_____

_____

_____

What a cat eats

_____

_____

_____

_____

Where a cat sleeps

_____

_____

_____

_____

 Find out more about cats. Add cat habits under the headings.

"Why Cat Eats First and Washes Afterward" and "Cat Habits," pages 82–88
Selection Comprehension: topic/main idea/details

47

Name _____

Sometimes 's or s' is added to a word to show that someone owns something. Read the sentence and the word in bold print. Add 's or s' to the word in bold print and write the word in the sentence.

cat's bowl

cats' bowls

1. **Emma**   Miss Kitty went to Aunt _____ house for lunch.

2. **aunt**   Miss Kitty thinks everything in her _____ house is hers.

3. **Kitty**   That chair is Miss _____ chair.

4. **cat**   Miss Kitty thinks the fuzzy toys are hers,

   but they are the three _____ toys.

5. **Drew**   That is cousin _____ blue sweater.

6. **boy**   Two _____ socks are on the floor.

7. **kitten**   Miss Kitty is trying to take food from those

   three small _____ bowls.

8. **friend**   Miss Kitty should learn that all her

   _____ lunches aren't hers!

 Write sentences to show that someone owns something. Use 's and s' .

"Why Cat Eats First and Washes Afterward" and "Cat Habits," pages 82–88
Decoding: possessives -'s, -s'

© D.C. Heath and Company

Name _____

Read these questions about Cat and Mouse and cat habits. Check (✓) the answer.

1. What problem did Mouse have?

   _____ Mouse had been caught by Cat.

   _____ Mouse had rude manners.

2. What did Mouse do to get away from Cat?

   _____ Mouse used his shadow to frighten Cat away.

   _____ Mouse used his head to trick Cat.

3. What does Cat do ever since Mouse tricked her?

   _____ Cat washes after she eats.

   _____ Cat does not talk to Mouse any more.

4. When there are no toys to play with, what do cats do?

   _____ They eat a mouse instead.

   _____ They pounce on anything that swings or moves.

5. Where do cats find warm places to sleep?

   _____ They sleep in sunny spots and under lamps.

   _____ Many cats go south in winter.

 How does a cat solve the problem of a dirty face? Write your answer in three sentences.

Name _____

Words at the top of a dictionary page are called guide words. They help you find a word. Read the word in bold print and the guide words. Circle the guide words that would be on the dictionary page.

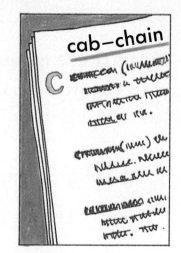
cab–chain

1. **catnip**

    climb—cloud   cab—chain   country—crate

2. **sun**

    swing—table   spoon—straw   summer—swim

3. **understand**

    umbrella—up   upset—us   until—use

4. **yawn**

    year—yellow   work—yard   wrong—zoom

5. **paw**

    pride—puzzle   page—pet   quack—sack

6. **beautiful**

    barn—cone   bird—burn   answer—basket

7. **habits**

    green—grown   house—hum   guess—happen

 Choose a set of guide words from this page. Write two words that you would find on a dictionary page with those guide words.

"Why Cat Eats First and Washes Afterward" and "Cat Habits," pages 82–88
Study Skills: reference sources (dictionary)

© D.C. Heath and Company

To show that someone owns something, add 's or s' to the word. Read this letter. Add 's or s' to the words with the lines after them.

September 17

Dear Mandy,

My sister ____ cat had a litter of kittens. We found

her under our neighbor ____ porch. It was our family ____

biggest surprise. All the kitten ____ fur is black. My sister

put a baby ____ blanket in a box to keep them warm. The

box is in Dad ____ workroom.

In a couple of weeks, she will give one kitten to

Mrs. Buffington for her twin son ____ seventh birthday. Do

you think Fred ____ cousin would also like a kitten?

Your friend,

David

 Look at the writing in your folder. Add 's or s' to words to show that someone owns something. Put the writing in your folder.

"Why Cat Eats First and Washes Afterward" and "Cat Habits," pages 81–88
Language: writing process (editing)

Name _____

Read this story about a wild kitten. Underline these words from "Follow Your Nose." Write the words with their meanings.

above	careful	noticed	softly
backwards	hungrily	rescue	

I was walking in the woods near our house when I noticed the wild kitten. She stared at me as she walked backwards a few steps. Then she turned and ran. Maybe she was scared when she saw a boy standing above her.

I got some milk for the kitten. I was careful not to get too close. I called softly to her so she would not be afraid. She lapped up the milk hungrily. I was afraid for her because it was very cold out. I knew if the weather grew worse I might have to rescue her again.

1. saw, paid attention to _____

2. taking care _____

3. in a higher place _____

4. in a way that shows a need for food _____

5. with the back end first _____

6. to save from harm or danger _____

7. in a low voice; quietly _____

 List three things that a cat would do softly and three things it would eat hungrily.

Each P sentence tells about a problem in "Follow Your Nose." Next to S, tell how the problem was solved. Write the page numbers for the answers.

1. **P** Jody's mom was too busy to play with him.

   S Jody _____ page _____

2. **P** Jody did not know where to go.

   S Jody's mom said, _____ page _____

3. **P** A worm was stuck on the sidewalk.

   S Jody _____ page _____

4. **P** Tomás could not get to his kitten.

   S Jody _____

   _____

   _____ page _____

5. **P** Jody did not have a friend to play with.

   S Jody _____

   _____

   _____ page _____

 Write another way Jody and Tomás could have gotten the kitten to come down.

_____

Name _____

Homophones are words that sound the same but have different meanings. Write the homophone that belongs in each sentence. Read the sentence again to check your word.

nose
knows

1. Tomás _____ it is fun to go for a walk.

2. When you follow your _____ , there are always fun things to see.

choose

3. Often he will _____ to walk in the woods.

chews

4. He likes to watch a caterpillar as it _____ leaves.

would
wood

5. One day Tomás saw a man chopping _____ .

6. He _____ like to know how to do that.

board
bored

7. Tomás walks on a _____ to cross the creek.

8. When he walks, he is never _____ .

you're
your

9. So get _____ sweater and go for a walk with Tomás.

10. I know that _____ going to have fun!

 Write homophones for these words: **pair, heel, meat.** Then use them in sentences.

**Knowing the order in which things happen
helps you remember them. Read the story.
Then number the sentences in order.**

Tomás put down something small in front of Panda. The
gift had pretty pink paper and bows on it. Panda wanted to
find out what it was. First she sniffed it. The gift smelled nice
to her. Next she hit it with her paw. But it stuck to a claw.
Then she shook her claw.

Panda was angry at the strange thing. She jumped on
the gift. She hit it over and over with her paws. Then she bit
it and shook it in her mouth. Something popped out—a
fuzzy toy mouse! At last, Panda carried the gift to her
pillow.

_____ Panda sniffed at the gift.

_____ Panda hit the gift with her paw.

_____ Panda carried the toy mouse to her pillow.

_____ Panda jumped on the gift.

_____ Tomás put something down in front of Panda.

_____ Panda shook her claw.

 Think of the steps you follow when you wrap a
gift. Write them in the correct order.

Writers think about ways they can publish, share, or change their writing. Choose some writing from your folder. Plan what you will do. Write your own ideas.

Publish

1. Draw pictures for the writing. Make a book with a cover.
2. Tape record the writing. Draw pictures to use with the recording.

3. My ideas _____

Share

1. Read the writing to classmates or other classes in school.
2. Put the writing on the bulletin board.

3. My ideas _____

Change

1. Write a different ending or change details in the writing.
2. Change the writing by making it a story, play or poem.

3. My ideas _____

What Will I Do?

_____

_____

_____

 Use the plan on this page to publish, share, or change the writing in your folder.

Name _____

Read the story. Write the words from "Too Much Noise" in the sentences. Read the story again to check your words.

creaks   squeaks   whistled
donkey   storyteller   wise
kettle   tea
noisy   village

Once upon a time, there was a small _____ .

A famous, wonderful _____ lived there in a tiny white cottage.

One day a stranger rode through the streets on a

_____ . The stranger _____ a song as he rode up to the storyteller's house.

The storyteller invited the stranger inside. He heated

water in a _____ over a fire to make some

hot _____ . Then he began to tell the stranger a story.

"Stop," said the stranger. "I hear _____ and

_____ . This house is loud and _____ !"

The storyteller was also a smart, _____ man.
He said to the stranger. "If you don't like the sounds in my house, you won't like the sound of my voice. You must learn to listen without making noise yourself."

 Write what you think the storyteller meant.

© D.C. Heath and Company

Name _____

This page tells what happened in "Too Much Noise." Read the sentence and the question. Check (✓) the answer.

1. Peter went to the village to see the wise man. What happened just before that?

   _____ Peter got a new hen.

   _____ Peter heard too many noises.

2. Peter got a sheep. What happened after Peter got a sheep?

   _____ Peter got a goat.

   _____ The sheep was too noisy.

3. Peter let the animals go. What happened just before that?

   _____ Peter went crazy.

   _____ Peter talked with the wise man again.

   What happened after the animals went away?

   _____ All the noises stopped.

   _____ The other noises seemed very quiet.

 Imagine that you hear a very loud dog barking late at night. Write four things that might happen.

© D.C. Heath and Company

"Too Much Noise," pages 100–111
Selection Comprehension: sequence

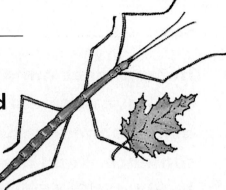

Each sentence has a silly word. Read the sentence. Use the clues to choose a real word for the sentence. Circle the word. Read the sentence with the real word.

1. The snow flea is a kind of <u>opprack</u> that is so small you cannot see it with your eyes. But the walking stick is one kind of <u>opprack</u> that is over a foot long!

    alligator   insect   elephant

2. When my kitten Snowball licks my cheek, it <u>swopples</u> me. I wonder if Snowball's mother <u>swopples</u> him when she licks his fur.

    tickles   tricks   flutters

3. The police officer told our class to check the <u>snozzer</u> carefully. I'm lucky that a red light near my house stops the <u>snozzer</u> so I can cross the street safely.

    turtle   turnips   traffic

4. When I eat pizza, I really need to use a <u>floop</u>. I use a <u>floop</u> to wipe the cheese off my chin.

    napkin   spoon   glass

5. The noise was like thunder when the elephant <u>dinnied</u>. As it <u>dinnied</u> at them, all the animals ran into the jungle.

    rested   charged   counted

 Write a sentence using a silly word. Give clues in the sentence. Have classmates guess the real word.

Name _____

Homophones are words that sound the same but have different meanings. Write the homophone that belongs in the sentence. Read the sentence again with your word.

eight, ate

1. Peter had _____ animals in his house.

wood, would

2. "I _____ like to give you some lunch," he said.

know, no

3. "But I do not _____ what you like to eat."

one, won

4. "I will eat _____ pan of popcorn," said the hen.

for, four

5. "I will eat _____ big oranges," said the pig.

here, hear

6. "I will eat a field of grass. Can you bring it

_____ for me?" asked the cow.

write, right

7. "I do not have the _____ food," said Peter.

buy, by

8. "I will go to town and _____ some."

 Choose three words you did not use and write sentences.

"Too Much Noise," pages 100–111
Vocabulary: homophones

Name _____

Read this story about a family who makes different kinds of music. Read each question and check (✓) the answer.

My brother Sam plays his drums every morning before breakfast. Then baby Kate bangs her spoon on the table. She giggles and laughs.

My name is Sue. I play the piano every afternoon after school. After I play, Mom and I laugh and dance together.

Then Dad comes home. He just smiles at us. He bought some ear plugs on the way home!

1. What happens first?
   _____ Sam plays his drums.
   _____ Sue plays the piano.

2. What happens right after Sam plays the drums?
   _____ Mom makes dinner.
   _____ Kate bangs her spoon.

3. When does Sue dance?
   _____ She dances before Kate bangs her spoon.
   _____ She dances after she plays the piano.

4. What happens last?
   _____ Dad smiles.
   _____ Dad gets some ear plugs.

 Circle the words in the story that are clues to the order in which things happened.

One section of the library has all the fiction books. These books are about make-believe things. Another section has nonfiction books. These books are about real things. This bookshelf has fiction and nonfiction books. Write the titles of the fiction books.

_____

_____

_____

_____

_____

 Write the titles of the nonfiction books.

_____

Read the story and underline the words in bold print. Then write the words with their meanings.

already monkey stairs
flight remember twenty

Do you like jokes and riddles? I know I do! My favorite joke is about a **monkey**. My biggest problem with jokes is that I can never **remember** them. Even if I've heard a joke **twenty** times, I still cannot remember it.

My friend Kelly told me a riddle that I thought I had **already** heard. She asked, "Why isn't it safe to keep a clock at the top of the **stairs**?"

"Because it might have too long a **flight**," I answered.

"No, that's a good answer, but it's wrong. The right answer is because it might run down and strike one!"

Will I remember that riddle to tell my friends?

1. ten plus ten _____

2. an animal with hair and paws _____

3. think of again _____

4. steps _____

5. by this time _____

6. set of steps that go up one floor _____

 Write a joke or riddle about monkeys.

_____

Look at these pictures from "Clowning Around."
Read the titles. Write a title under each picture.

- **Getting Ready**
- **Riding High**
- **Being Sad**

- **The Red Wig and Top Hat**
- **Doing Tricks**

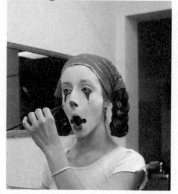

1. _____

2. _____

3. _____

4. _____

5. _____

 Choose one title and tell what is happening in
the picture.

_____

Read the words in each row. Circle the word with the same vowel sound as the word in bold print. (Leave the lines blank for now.)

1.	**how**	bought	mouth	_____
2.	**walk**	paw	plate	_____
3.	**king**	strike	string	_____
4.	**cost**	saw	plow	_____
5.	**sea**	freeze	height	_____
6.	**kind**	wrist	blind	_____
7.	**head**	sweat	swan	_____
8.	**steak**	speed	weigh	_____
9.	**lie**	flight	list	_____
10.	**book**	touch	put	_____
11.	**cold**	slow	growl	_____
12.	**chief**	weed	spread	_____

Read the story. Look at each underlined word. Match it to a word in bold print with the same vowel sound. Write the underlined words on the lines above.

How <u>would</u> you <u>like</u> to go to a magic show? I've <u>already</u> <u>bought</u> the tickets <u>because</u> they were almost all sold.

The man in the show can do many tricks. <u>He</u> can guess your <u>height</u> and <u>weight</u>. He can change a <u>piece</u> of <u>string</u> into a scarf. Then he <u>unfolds</u> the scarf and a rabbit pops <u>out</u>. He juggles spoons and not one hits the floor.

 Write the words in bold print as headings. List other story words with the same vowel sound.

_____

As you read this story about Alligator and Cat, think about the order in which things happen. Then number the sentences in order.

Alligator and Cat were playing hide-and-seek. First Alligator counted while Cat hid. Cat hid high in a tree. Then Alligator went to find Cat. He looked in the mud near the pond and in the tall grass. He could not find Cat.

"Here I am," said Cat, "up in the tree."

"That's not fair," said Alligator. "I can't climb a tree."

After climbing down from the tree, Cat counted while Alligator hid. Then Cat went to find Alligator, but he could not find him.

Where is Alligator?

☐ Cat hid in a tree.

☐ Alligator went to find Cat.

☐ Alligator counted while Cat hid.

☐ Cat counted while Alligator hid.

☐ Alligator and Cat played hide-and-seek.

 Where do you think Alligator is hiding?
Write your answer at the end of the story.

Read each list of words. Circle the list that is in ABC order.

1. | chief | card | card | clown |
clown	chief	clown	count
card	clown	chief	card
count	count	count	chief

2. | hung | heard | hiss | hard |
hiss	hung	hard	heard
heard	hiss	hung	hiss
hard	hard	heard	hung

3. | laugh | laugh | lock | lunch |
lunch	lick	lunch	lick
lick	lock	lick	laugh
lock	lunch	laugh	lock

4. | facts | felt | facts | felt |
felt	field	felt	flat
field	facts	flat	facts
flat	flat	field	field

5. | geese | goose | glad | geese |
growl	geese	goose	glad
glad	growl	geese	goose
goose	glad	growl	growl

 List in ABC order five animals you would like to see in a circus.

Words at the top of a dictionary page can help you find a word. Read each word in bold print and the pairs of guide words. Choose the guide words for the word in bold print. Fill in the circle.

1. **clown**
   - ○ cage—city
   - ○ chief—cranberry
   - ○ cute—door

2. **seal**
   - ○ rush—sale
   - ○ silly—skirt
   - ○ sack—shop

3. **elephant**
   - ○ cross—den
   - ○ end—farm
   - ○ earth—fence

4. **tiger**
   - ○ stripe—table
   - ○ sweater—toad
   - ○ trunk—tusk

5. **bear**
   - ○ away—bird
   - ○ brook—butterfly
   - ○ ant—balloon

6. **dog**
   - ○ dance—do
   - ○ dock—doll
   - ○ cub—dirt

7. **stairs**
   - ○ sleep—small
   - ○ tail—town
   - ○ soup—stone

 Choose a set of guide words from this page. Write two words that you would find on a dictionary page with those guide words.

_____

Some words from "Heather's Feathers" are used in these sentences. Read the sentences and the word meanings. Underline the word that matches the meaning.

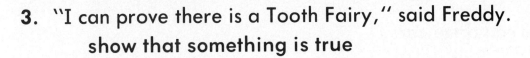

1. Heather had not seen the Tooth Fairy so she did not believe in her.

   think something is true

2. "There is a Tooth Fairy," said Robbie. "She left a present for me under my pillow."

   something given to another person

3. "I can prove there is a Tooth Fairy," said Freddy.

   show that something is true

4. But Freddy could not prove it because he still had all of his teeth.

   for a reason

5. Robbie would lose a loose tooth that same day.

   not have any longer

6. None of Heather's teeth had fallen out because she had no teeth!

   not any

7. Heather looked at all the feathers on the ground. She knew she was molting.

   dropping feathers before new ones grow

 When do birds and animals **molt**? Look in a dictionary or encyclopedia to find out.

Name _____

This page tells about "Heather's Feathers."
Read the sentence. If it tells something real,
write **R**. If it tells something make-believe,
write **M**.

1. _____ Birds have feathers.

2. _____ Birds have beaks.

3. _____ Birds can paint pictures with their wings.

4. _____ Teeth can fall out when you are eating.

5. _____ Birds can bake cakes.

6. _____ Birds can drive cars.

7. _____ Birds are molting when they lose their feathers.

8. _____ Bright new feathers grow in when a bird loses
its old ones.

**Write a sentence that tells something real
about birds. Use the story to help you.**

_____

_____

_____

_____

 Have you ever lost a tooth? Write or tell
what happened.

"Heather's Feathers," pages 140–149
Selection Comprehension: reality-fantasy

© D.C. Heath and Company

Name _____

The letters <u>oi</u>, <u>ou</u>, <u>ow</u>, and <u>oy</u> stand for different vowel sounds. Read the sentences and the words in bold print. Circle the word that belongs in the sentence. Read the sentence with your word.

1. When Heather loses her feathers, she shouts for _____ .
          found   prowl   joy

2. At other times, Heather is careful not to make _____ .
         blouse   noise   frown

3. When she hears a cat _____ , Heather stays quiet.
         meow   drown   coil

4. Heather knows what the cat would _____ for dinner.
         join   enjoy   growl

5. She doesn't _____ the cat to get too close.
         allow   about   around

6. Heather hopes she can _____ the cat's dinner.
         bounce   spoil   toy

7. A mouse runs across the _____ near the cat.
         scowl   cloud   ground

8. The cat _____ on it and will eat the mouse for dinner.
         bows   pounces   browses

 Write four headings: <u>oi</u>, <u>ou</u>, <u>ow</u>, <u>oy</u>. Under each heading, write the words on this page with the same vowel sound.

Name _____

Antonyms are words with opposite meanings. Read each pair of sentences. Look at the underlined word. Circle the antonym in the second sentence for the underlined word.

1. Heather thought she <u>hated</u> being a bird.
   When she molted, she loved being a bird.

2. Heather lost her <u>dull</u> feathers.
   Her new ones were bright and pretty.

3. Heather liked to fly <u>over</u> the bridge.
   Sometimes she flew under it to prove that she could.

4. Heather could fly <u>high</u> above the trees.
   When she molted, she stayed low to the ground.

Write each word with its antonym.

all   before   lose   remember   tighter
above   close   louder   tallest   worse

1. find _____   6. looser _____

2. better _____   7. below _____

3. none _____   8. far _____

4. after _____   9. softer _____

5. forget _____   10. shortest _____

 Choose a pair of antonyms from this page.
Write them in sentences.

_____

© D.C. Heath and Company

Stories tell about real and make-believe things. This story is part real and part make-believe. Read the story. Then underline the sentences that tell about real things.

The bird's new feathers were beautiful. There were bright yellow feathers on its tail, shiny black ones on its head, and frosty white feathers on its throat. The bird flew about the forest trying out its new feathers.

"Look at my beautiful new feathers," the bird shouted to the squirrel. "Your dull gray fur isn't as pretty as my new feathers."

"Look at the sunny yellow feathers in my tail," the bird chirped to the toad. "Your skin is ugly and bumpy."

One day all the forest animals were at the stream getting a drink. The bird flew there to join them. But the animals ran back into the forest.

"Why won't you play with me?" asked the bird. "I am more beautiful than ever before."

"You brag too much," the other animals said. "Being beautiful is not as important as being a friend."

 Circle the sentences that tell about make-believe things.

Name _____

These sentences need details to be clearer. Use the words in the box or your own in place of the underlined words. Write the new sentences.

- pink and white marble
- an enormous nest
- all the birds in the land
- in a beautiful palace
- colorful feathers

---

1. The feather fairy lived <u>there</u>.

_____

2. It was made of <u>something</u>.

_____

3. Huge piles of <u>them</u> filled a room in the tower.

_____

_____

4. Soon the feather fairy would make <u>something</u> from them.

_____

_____

5. <u>They</u> could visit her wonderful creation.

_____

 Share your writing in class. Then take the writing from your folder and add information to make it clearer. Put the writing in your folder.

"Heather's Feathers," pages 140–149
Language: writing process (revising)

Name _____

Read this story. Write the words from "Animal Teeth" in the sentences. Then read the story again to check your words.

beaver   important   tusks
bottom   lion   walrus
grinding   polar bear

Let's play a guessing game about animals. I will tell you

some _____ facts. Then you guess the animal.

The first animal is white and furry. It lives in cold places

where there is a lot of ice and snow. It is a _____ .

You might see the next animal sitting on top of an

iceberg. It has special teeth called _____ . It is a

_____ .

The third animal is brown and furry. It uses its teeth for

chopping and _____ trees to make a home. Its

home is often built in a pond or stream. It is a _____ .

The last animal is a large kind of cat. It uses its sharp

top and _____ teeth for chewing meat. It is a

_____ .

 Choose an animal and tell an important fact about it. Have classmates guess what it is.

You read how animals use their teeth in "Animal Teeth." Write each animal's name where it belongs in the chart. Then answer the questions.

beaver	cow	elephant	horse	walrus
cat	dog	giraffe	lion	wolf

How Animals Use Their Teeth				
To Eat Meat	To Eat Plants	To Fight	To Move Around	To Do Work

1. Why do dogs, lions, cats, and wolves need

   sharp teeth? _____

2. In what ways besides eating do some animals

   use their teeth? _____

3. Which animal uses its teeth for fighting and

   moving? _____

 Add other animal names to the chart. Discuss your ideas with classmates.

© D.C. Heath and Company

"Animal Teeth," pages 150–153
Selection Comprehension: topic/main idea/details

Homophones are words that sound the same but have different meanings. Read each sentence and the homophones. Write the homophone that belongs in the sentence. Read the sentence to check your word.

wood
would

1. Mrs. Ring did not have any _____ .

_____

four
for

2. She needed some _____ the stove.

_____

hole
whole

3. "We must have enough for the _____ winter," she said.

_____

son
sun

4. Mrs. Ring asked her _____ Lee to go into the forest.

_____

dear
deer

5. A herd of _____ watched him as he walked down the path.

_____

by
buy

6. Lee found many logs _____ a tiny stream.

_____

rose
rows

7. Later, he stacked them in _____ beside the house.

_____

 Write sentences for the words that you did not write on the lines.

_____

© D.C. Heath and Company

Name _____

Stories are about real and make-believe things. This story is part real and part make-believe. Read the story and answer the questions.

The day began with a sharp, cold wind. The polar bear put on his hat and buttoned up his coat. He climbed up on an iceberg to get out of the freezing water. A walrus used its tusks to get on the iceberg too.

The polar bear didn't want to share the iceberg. He told the walrus to go away. The walrus cried as he slid sadly back into the water and swam away.

1. Which three things in the story could really happen?

_____

_____

_____

2. Which three things in the story are make-believe?

_____

_____

_____

 Tell one real and one make-believe thing about a polar bear.

"Animal Teeth," pages 150–153
Comprehension: reality-fantasy

Name _____

In "Animal Teeth," you read about different kinds of animal teeth. Write the words under the headings.

cat   eat   grind   wolf
chop   elephant   horse   work
cow   fight   lion
dog   giraffe   walrus

Animals With Tusks

_____

_____

Animals With Flat Teeth

_____

_____

Animals With Sharp Teeth

_____

_____

_____

How Animals Use Their Teeth

_____

_____

_____

 Write the heading **Animals With Large Front Teeth.** Write the names of animals with large front teeth.

The writer of this story wants to show that the action has already happened. Read the story and circle the verbs that are correct. Then write the correct verbs over the underlined verbs. Read the story with your changes.

I always thought my uncle's farm <u>is</u> a quiet place. But

when I visited him last week, I <u>learn</u> how noisy it really was.

Horses <u>neigh</u> loudly and <u>gallop</u> across the pastures.

Their hooves <u>clomp</u> over the hard earth. The cows mooed in

the fields and <u>chomp</u> on the wet spring grass. Geese <u>cackle</u>

in the barnyard and turkeys <u>gobble</u> the grain. Pigs oinked

for their slops and <u>wallow</u> in the mud.

In spite of the noise, I fell asleep under an oak tree

while an owl <u>hoots</u> in the branches.

Discuss the verb changes. Which verbs did not change? Why? Check the writing in your folder. If the action has already happened, write the verbs with <u>d</u> or <u>ed</u>.

"Animal Teeth," pages 150–153
Language: writing process (editing)

Name _____

Some words from "Molly and the Slow Teeth" are used in these sentences. Read each pair of sentences. Underline the word in the first sentence that matches the underlined meaning in the second sentence.

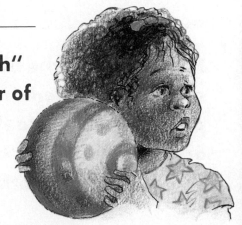

1. Molly was sure that she would lose her first tooth soon.
   She felt <u>certain</u> that it would happen any day now.

2. Molly had already learned a way to lose a tooth.
   She <u>found out</u> about it from her friend Marvin.

3. Marvin said, "Tie your tooth to a doorknob with string.
   Any <u>round door handle</u> can be used."

4. "I think I'll try that trick tonight," thought Molly.
   "I will get some string <u>this very night</u>."

5. Molly's father told her not to worry about her teeth.
   The problem of how to lose a tooth <u>troubled</u> Molly.

6. While she was reading her dinosaur book, Molly pushed her tongue against her tooth.
   She wondered if these <u>animals of long, long ago</u> had trouble with their teeth.

7. Molly hoped that the Tooth Fairy would leave a quarter.
   She needed <u>twenty-five cents</u> to buy a bookmark at the school fair.

 Quarter also means one of four parts or ¼.
Draw a pie and cut it into four equal parts.
Color ¼ of the pie.

In "Molly and the Slow Teeth," Molly tried to solve her problem in different ways. Read the problem and write the solutions. Circle good or bad to tell what kind of an idea it was. Then tell why you think so.

Problem: Molly wanted a loose tooth.

Solution #1: _____

_____

_____

Good or Bad Idea?

Why? _____

_____

Solution #2: _____

_____

_____

Good or Bad Idea?

Why? _____

_____

Solution #3: _____

_____

_____

Good or Bad Idea?

Why? _____

_____

Solution #4: _____

_____

_____

Good or Bad Idea?

Why? _____

_____

 Write or tell a story about the time you lost your first tooth.

"Molly and the Slow Teeth," pages 154–165
Selection Comprehension: problem-solution

Name _____

When you want to show that someone owns something, you add 's or s' to the word. Read the sentence and the word in bold print. Write the word with 's or s'. Read the sentence to check your word.

1. Susan   It was _____ turn to visit the dentist, and her two sisters went along.

2. dentist   Many _____ offices were in the same building.

3. brother   Susan brought her _____ books to read while she waited.

4. Mrs. Brown   _____ dentist told her about Susan's loose teeth.

5. sister   Susan's two _____ teeth were also loose.

6. friend   That night, Susan borrowed her best _____ tooth pillow.

7. Tooth Fairy   She wondered what the _____ present would be.

8. girl   Would it be as nice as all the other _____ presents?

 Write sentences using words with 's and s'.

© D.C. Heath and Company

"Molly and the Slow Teeth," pages 154–165
Decoding: possessives –'s,–s'

Name _____

Synonyms are words that have the same or almost the same meaning. Read each pair of sentences. Look at the underlined word. Circle the synonym in the second sentence for the underlined word in the first sentence.

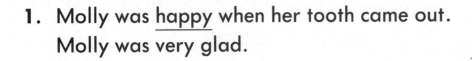

1. Molly was <u>happy</u> when her tooth came out.
   Molly was very glad.

2. Molly's new tooth was <u>small</u>.
   It was so tiny that she could hardly see it.

3. Molly's friends <u>laughed</u> when she told them about it.
   They giggled at the funny way Molly lost her tooth.

4. Molly told them about the Tooth Fairy's <u>present</u>.
   She left a gift under Molly's pillow.

_____

Write the synonym for each word.

large   scared   grin   fast   loud   pretty

1. smile _____

2. quick _____

3. afraid _____

4. noisy _____

5. beautiful _____

6. big _____

 Write two sentences with words that are synonyms.
Ask a classmate to circle the synonyms.

"Molly and the Slow Teeth," pages 154–165
Vocabulary: synonyms

Name _____

**Read this story about Molly and her sister.
Then answer the questions.**

Lilly was happy when Molly's tooth came out. She was also a little worried. Lilly still had all her baby teeth.

One day Lilly took a large ham bone and went out to sit on the steps in front of her apartment building. Molly walked by and asked, "What are you doing?"

"Chewing on a bone," said Lilly, "to make my teeth loose."

"Your teeth will come out in time," said Molly.

"I guess you're right," said Lilly. She threw the bone in the trash can.

"Let's get an apple," said Molly.

1. Who is in the story? _____

2. Where does the story take place? _____

_____

3. What does Lilly want? _____

4. What three things does Lilly do in the story? _____

_____

5. What happens at the end? _____

_____

 Write sentences telling what Molly and Lilly are like.

_____

Name _____

Read the story. Then read the sentences that tell what happened. Write sentences that tell why.

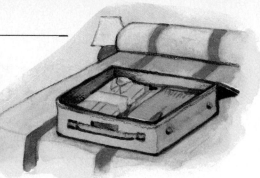

On the first day of summer vacation, Marvin woke up early because he was going somewhere special.

Marvin's mother drove him to the airport so that he could take a plane to his grandfather's. Marvin wanted to be safe, so he buckled his seat belt on the plane. Soon Marvin wanted to take a nap, so he asked for a pillow and blanket.

Marvin ran when he got off the plane because he could see his grandfather waiting at the gate.

1. Marvin woke up early. Why? _____

_____

2. Marvin's mother drove him to the airport. Why? _____

_____

_____

3. Marvin buckled his seat belt. Why? _____

_____

4. Marvin asked for a pillow and blanket. Why? _____

_____

5. Marvin ran. Why? _____

 Write what happens next and why.

_____

© D.C. Heath and Company

"Molly and the Slow Teeth," pages 154–165
Comprehension: cause-effect

**Read this story. Write the words from
"The Lion and the Mouse" in the sentences.
Then read the story to check your words.**

eyes	lazily	thrashing
happily	Often	tiny
hardly	repay	trouble

Most mice are _____ , but Morris was a huge

mouse. _____ , Morris slept in a bed that was

too small. Some nights, Morris _____ slept. He

was tired of _____ around in a little bed. So
Morris asked his sister Jenny to help him find a bigger bed.

Jenny said, "It won't be any _____ to find
you a bigger bed." So Jenny got Morris a bigger bed.
   That night Morris fell asleep right away. The next

morning, he woke up slowly and _____ . He

rubbed his big brown _____ . He smiled

_____ and said to Jenny, "How can I ever

_____ you for finding me a new bed?"

Write the root words for **happily, hardly,
lazily, thrashing.**

Name _____

Think about the order of things that happened in "The Lion and the Mouse." Read the sentences in the box. Write each sentence in order with the numbered sentences.

> • The lion was caught in a net.
> • The lion caught the mouse in his paw.
> • The mouse had repaid the lion.
> • The lion laughed and let the mouse go.

1. A mouse ran across a sleeping lion's nose.

2. _____

3. The mouse said she would repay the lion if he let her go.

4. _____

5. _____

6. The mouse chewed through the ropes of the net.

7. _____

 Write a sentence telling something nice you could do to help a friend.

© D.C. Heath and Company

"The Lion and the Mouse," pages 168–173
Selection Comprehension: sequence

Name _____

Some words on this page have the vowel sounds in <u>caught</u> and <u>found</u>. Read each sentence. Underline the word that belongs in the sentence. Read the sentence with your word.

1. Baby Paul wakes up at _____ every morning.
   cause   dawn   fault

2. He _____, or cries, until someone gets up.
   bawls   taught   draws

3. Mom puts a _____ on her shoulders and picks him up.
   cauliflower   faucet   shawl

4. Paul is not the only one making _____ in the morning.
   sounds   bounds   clowns

5. We have a _____ dog that barks and begs to go out.
   ground   town   hound

6. Her name is Chocolate because she is _____.
   round   loud   brown

7. Another noise is our neighbor mowing his _____.
   brow   lawn   powder

8. The only way I have quiet is to turn my radio up loud to _____ out all the noise.
   drown   bawl   draw

 Write four words that rhyme with **claw**. Then write four words that rhyme with **cow**.

"The Lion and the Mouse," pages 168–173
Decoding: vowel diphthongs <u>aw</u>, <u>au</u>, <u>ou</u>, <u>ow</u>

Name _____

Synonyms are words that have the same or almost the same meaning. Read each sentence and circle two words that are synonyms.

1. Martha is just a small butterfly with tiny wings.

2. She flutters from one flower to another and lands on a pretty pink blossom.

3. Martha has an insect friend, but her best pal is Fred the giraffe.

4. Fred is so tall that he can reach the leaves on very high tree branches.

5. Fred likes to eat the fresh green grass and chew the juicy leaves.

6. Martha can trace Fred's steps and follow him anywhere.

7. When Martha has any trouble, she tells her problem to Fred.

8. Once she needed to be rescued from danger, and Fred saved her.

9. When Fred naps, Martha sleeps on one of Fred's horns.

10. While the two friends sleep, it is very quiet and still.

 Write sentences using these pairs of synonyms: frightened/scared, fast/quick.

"The Lion and the Mouse," pages 168–173
Vocabulary: synonyms

This page tells about "The Lion and the Mouse." Read the sentences that tell what happened. Write sentences that tell why. Use your book to find the page number for the answers.

1. The lion woke up. Why? _____

_____ page _____

2. The lion lifted his paw. Why? _____

_____ page _____

3. The lion laughed. Why? _____

_____ page _____

4. The lion let the mouse go. Why? _____

_____ page _____

5. The mouse could not go near the net. Why? _____

_____ page _____

6. The lion was able to get out of the net. Why? _____

_____

_____ page _____

Write three reasons why a lion might get angry.

Name _____

Read this story about how Grandmother Hen solved a problem. Then answer the questions.

Grandmother Hen was growing berries. She would bake special cakes for the chickens. But a raccoon was eating all her berries.

Grandfather Rooster said, "Put a fence with nails around the berries. The nails will keep the raccoon out."

"No," said Grandmother Hen. "I don't want to be mean to him." So she said to the raccoon, "Please stay away from my berries. If you do, I will give you some of my cakes."

The raccoon thanked Grandmother Hen. The next time he ate the berries, they were baked in a cake.

1. What was Grandmother Hen's problem?

_____

2. What did Grandfather Rooster want to do about the problem?

_____

3. Why didn't Grandmother Hen like his idea?

_____

4. How did Grandmother Hen finally solve her problem?

_____

_____

 Make a list of other ways Grandmother Hen might have solved her problem.

© D.C. Heath and Company

Name _____

**Read this story about whales. Then read
the story again and underline the words
in bold print. Last, write the words beside
their meanings.**

healthy   ocean   whales

heart   remember

Two whales live in a huge tank at our zoo.
As they swim under the water, they are very beautiful
to watch.

The zoo vet takes care of the whales. She swims in the
tank and checks each whale's heart. The whales must be
given lots of care to stay healthy and happy. After all, the
tank is very different from the ocean where they were born.

I remember reading about whales in school. I was
surprised to learn that they are not a kind of fish. They
breathe air just as we do. They also sing as we do.

1. large sea animals that must have air to breathe _____

2. well, not sick _____

3. part of the body that pumps blood _____

4. a large body of salt water _____

5. to think of again _____

 Make a list of four things a vet might do for
other animals.

_____

Read the headings and think about the facts in "Animal Helpers." Write the facts under the headings. Use your book to help you.

Vets

help your pet get better

_____

_____

_____

Zookeepers

clean cages

_____

_____

Ocean Animal Helpers

help whales, sharks, and seals

_____

_____

_____

Forest Rangers

_____

_____

_____

What You Can Do

take good care of your pet

_____

_____

_____

 What things can people do to take good care of their pets? Make a list.

_____

© D.C. Heath and Company

"Animal Helpers," pages 174–179
Selection Comprehension: topic/main idea/details

Name _____

The words in bold print have more than one meaning. Read the story. Write the words in the sentences. Use each word twice. Read the story again to check your words.

back	bed	fly
bark	fair	play

It was a _____, sunny day. Jimmy watered

the flowers in his flower _____. Later Jimmy and

his dog walked to the county _____ to see the

animals and the clowns. At the fair, Jimmy saw the clowns

act in a _____ .

On the way home, Jimmy's dog ran _____ to

_____ at a bird in a tree. The dog's barking

made the bird _____ higher into the tree. The

dog scratched the _____ of the tree with its

claws. Jimmy yelled, "Don't chase the bird. I'll

_____ a game with you."

That night Jimmy was tired. His _____ and

his feet hurt. Although a _____ buzzed around

his head, Jimmy fell sound asleep in his _____ .

 Write sentences using other words with
more than one meaning.

Read these sentences about bears. Then answer the questions about the topic, main idea, and details.

There are many kinds of bears. One kind is the brown bear. It is one of the biggest bears in the world. Brown bears grow to be 9 feet tall and weigh more than 1,500 pounds. Another kind of bear is the grizzly bear. Grizzlies get angry quickly. They can be very dangerous. Grizzlies grow to be 8 feet tall and weigh about 800 pounds.

1. What is the topic? (What are these sentences about?)

_____

2. What is the main idea? (What is the most important idea in these sentences?)

_____

3. What two facts or details tell about the main idea?

_____

_____

 Draw a picture of one kind of bear. Under the picture, write two sentences that tell about the bear.

Name _____

**Read the words and the headings.
Write the words that belong together
under each heading.**

bears   forest   rabbits   sharks   zoo
clams   litter   rangers   skunks   zookeepers
fire   ocean   seals   vets

Where Animals Live

_____

_____

_____

Animal Helpers

_____

_____

_____

Animals Found in the Forest

_____

_____

_____

Animals Found in the Ocean

_____

_____

_____

Things That Hurt Animals

_____

_____

 Add other words under each heading.

A telling sentence and a command end with a period. A question ends with a question mark. An exclamation ends with an exclamation mark. Read this story. Draw a line through each wrong punctuation mark. Write the correct punctuation mark beside it.

What fun it is to work at the zoo? Would you like to help me!   Come into the chimp house with me.   What a cute baby chimp that is?   Please feed it this banana.   Don't put your fingers near the cage?   Mother chimps bite hard.   Now follow me to the snake house?   Please hand me the key!   Watch out.   A snake is out of its cage.   Can you see it anywhere!   There it is.   Come down out of that tree?   Now let's feed the elephants.

 Discuss the punctuation changes. Which punctuation marks did not change? Why? Look at the writing in your folder. Check the kinds of sentences and correct the punctuation marks.

Name _____

These sentences use words from "Señor Billy Goat." Read the sentence and the word meaning. Underline the word that matches the meaning.

1. My grandmother is blind, but she helps our family a lot.

   not able to see

2. She likes to do things, and she is always busy.

   having a lot to do

3. Grandma and her husband have been married for 51 years.

   a man who has a wife

4. Grandma and Grandpa promised to make a big garden this summer.

   said they would do something

5. They will plant vegetables like carrots, beans, and corn.

   plants with parts that are good to eat

6. I will grow lettuce that will taste as sweet as sugar.

   a plant with big green leaves that are good to eat

7. Grandma says that I am young, but I can help in the garden.

   not old

 Rewrite the sentences on this page using the word meaning instead of the word.

Name _____

Think about the order in which things happened in "Señor Billy Goat." Read the sentences in the box. Write each sentence in the order in which things happened in the story.

- The ant bit the goat all over.
- The goat chased Ramón.
- María and Ramón gave the ant flour and sugar.
- The goat ran at her.

---

1. Ramón saw a billy goat in the vegetable garden.

2. _____

3. María tried to talk to the goat.

4. _____

5. An ant promised to help them.

6. _____

7. The goat rolled down the hill.

8. _____

 What do you think the ant will do next? Share your answer with your classmates.

© D.C. Heath and Company

"Señor Billy Goat," pages 180–191
Selection Comprehension: sequence

Name _____

An ending added to a word can change the meaning of the word. Add <u>ly</u> to each word in bold print. Remember to change <u>y</u> to <u>i</u> in some words. Write the word in the sentence. Read the sentence again to check your word.

lazy   **1.** One day, Ramón was napping _____ in the sun.

careful   **2.** María walked by _____ so she would not wake him.

happy   **3.** "He looks so peaceful," she thought _____.

sudden   **4.** _____, a terrible sound woke Ramón up.

noisy   **5.** A plane roared _____ overhead.

close   **6.** Ramón and María followed it _____ with their eyes.

quick   **7.** She turned and walked _____ to the barn.

angry   **8.** "Even the goats raise their heads when the planes fly by," María said _____.

 Write the root words for tinier and noisiest.

Name _____

Read the sentences and the meanings of the underlined words. Think about the meaning of the word that is used in the sentence. Circle the letter before the correct meaning.

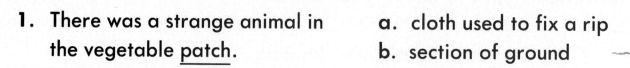

1. There was a strange animal in the vegetable <u>patch</u>.
   a. cloth used to fix a rip
   b. section of ground

2. A <u>quarter</u> of the patch was trampled down.
   a. twenty-five cents
   b. one fourth of something

3. Broken stakes and other <u>litter</u> covered the ground.
   a. little bits of trash
   b. animals born together

4. "Maybe it's a bird, not an animal!" cried Ramón. "Is it a <u>crane</u>?"
   a. machine for lifting things
   b. bird with long legs

5. "Cranes are small," said María. "That animal weighs 100 <u>pounds</u>."
   a. places to keep animals
   b. amount of weight

6. "It's not an elephant," said Ramón. "It doesn't have a <u>trunk</u>."
   a. chest to keep things in
   b. long nose or snout

7. "The animal in the garden has <u>horns</u>!" said María.
   a. hard, pointed growths
   b. noisemakers on cars

8. "I know!" said Ramón. "That animal in our <u>yard</u> is a goat!"
   a. three feet
   b. ground around a house

 Think of two meanings for the words ruler and cast. Use your dictionary if you need help.

© D.C. Heath and Company

"Señor Billy Goat," pages 180–191
Vocabulary: multiple meanings

Name _____

Read this story. Think about the characters and what happens. Answer the questions.

Señor Billy Goat was mean to the other animals on the farm. He pushed the chickens and chased the cows away. Then he ate their food. "That goat does not know how to share," said Great Horse. "We will teach him a lesson."

While the goat slept, the animals put a fence around him. They put cans and papers with the goat.

When Señor Billy Goat woke up, he was very hungry. But there was only junk. That's why, even to this day, goats will eat just about anything.

1. What was Señor Billy Goat like?

_____

2. What three important things happened in the story?

_____

_____

_____

3. What lesson did Señor Billy Goat learn?

_____

_____

 Where does this story take place?

_____

"Señor Billy Goat," pages 180–191
Comprehension: character traits/setting/plot

Think about what is real and what is make-believe in "Señor Billy Goat." Write R next to the sentences that could really happen. Write M next to the sentences that are make-believe.

1. _____ A little old woman and old man lived in Puerto Rico.

2. _____ A billy goat came to eat in their garden.

3. _____ "I have come to help you," the ant whispered.

4. _____ Ramón patted the billy goat and said, "Hello."

5. _____ The billy goat went at Ramón with his horns all set.

6. _____ The ant asked for a little sack of flour.

7. _____ The ant went through a crack in the floor.

8. _____ "Ouch! Ouch! I have stepped on an ant hill," the billy goat cried.

9. _____ The ant crawled up the goat's leg and back.

10. _____ "I can make Señor Billy Goat go away," said the ant.

 Look in the story. Write one more thing about the ant that is real. Write one more thing that is make-believe.

Name _____

Read this story. Write the words from "Clocks and More Clocks" in the sentences. Read the story to check your words.

attic   correct
bought   o'clock
Clockmaker   splendid   Wonderful

Mr. Higgins had many clocks, but he wanted one that

was special. He asked the _____ to make him

the most _____ clock in the whole world.

Mr. Higgins said, "My clock must always tell the

_____ time. Loud bells should ring when a

new hour passes. It should ring twelve times when it is

twelve _____ . I want to hear time passing

even when I am upstairs in the _____ ."

The Clockmaker said, "You will only hear the hours
passing. I will make you a clock that goes ding every
minute and ding-a-ling every hour."

"_____", said Mr. Higgins. He

_____ the clock. He listens to it all the

time because he doesn't want to miss a minute!

 Circle two new words on this page that are
synonyms. Write four pairs of synonyms of
your own.

Name _____

This page tells about "Clocks and More
Clocks." Read each sentence that tells what
happened in the story. Then write a sentence
to tell why it happened.

1. Mr. Higgins found a clock. Why? _____

_____

2. Mr. Higgins bought a clock for the bedroom. Why? _____

_____

3. Mr. Higgins bought more clocks. Why? _____

_____

4. Each clock told a different time. Why? _____

_____

_____

5. The Clockmaker went to Mr. Higgins's house. Why? _____

_____

_____

6. Mr. Higgins bought a watch. Why? _____

_____

_____

 Tell how you use clocks everyday.

_____

© D.C. Heath and Company

"Clocks and More Clocks," pages 194–202
Selection Comprehension: cause-effect

Some words have more than one meaning. Read the sentence. Fill in the circle beside the meaning for the underlined word. Then write a sentence using the other meaning.

1. Mr. Higgins put his clock on a large <u>chest</u> in the shop.
   - ○ the body part below the neck
   - ○ a box with a lid

   _____

2. The Clockmaker took off the <u>face</u> of the clock.
   - ○ the front part of the head
   - ○ the front part of a timepiece

   _____

3. "I will have to <u>check</u> the clock to see what is wrong with it," said the Clockmaker.
   - ○ look at carefully
   - ○ a kind of mark

   _____

4. "One of the <u>hands</u> was stuck," said the Clockmaker. "But it works just fine now."
   - ○ the parts of the body that have fingers
   - ○ the parts of the clock that point to the correct time

 Write a sentence using the word **fan.** Then write two meanings for **fan.** Have a classmate tell which meaning is used in the sentence.

Name _____

Sometimes a writer gives clues to help you know what is not in the story. Read this story and the questions. Check (✓) the answers.

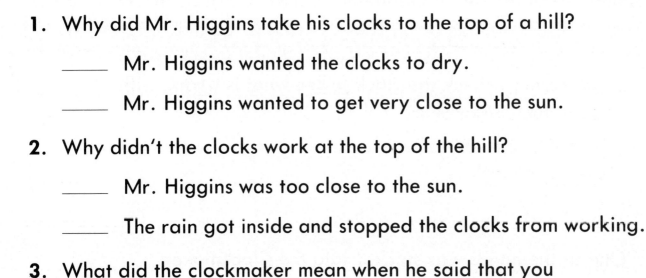

The clockmaker told Mr. Higgins that he could tell time by the sun. "Watch the sun as it moves across the sky," he said. Mr. Higgins took his clocks to a hill. As he climbed, it started to rain. Water ran down the faces of the clocks.

When Mr. Higgins reached the top, he was close to the sun. The clocks were covered with water and they weren't ticking. "The clockmaker is wrong," said Mr. Higgins. "You cannot tell time by the sun at all."

1. Why did Mr. Higgins take his clocks to the top of a hill?

    _____ Mr. Higgins wanted the clocks to dry.

    _____ Mr. Higgins wanted to get very close to the sun.

2. Why didn't the clocks work at the top of the hill?

    _____ Mr. Higgins was too close to the sun.

    _____ The rain got inside and stopped the clocks from working.

3. What did the clockmaker mean when he said that you could tell time by the sun?

    _____ You can guess the time if you are near the sun.

    _____ The sun's place in the sky helps tell the time.

 Think about the clues that helped you answer each question. Underline the clues in the story.

Name _____

The title page and the table of contents are at the beginning of a book. Look at these pages. Then answer the questions.

Title Page

How Clocks Work
by
Max Higgins

Pictures by
James Wilson

1987 by
Hourglass Press

Table of Contents

1. On which page is the author's name? _____

2. Which page tells what the chapters are about?

    _____

3. Who drew the pictures? _____

4. In which chapter can you read about new clocks? _____

5. Which page tells when the book was printed? _____

6. Which chapter tells how to build a clock? _____

7. Which chapter tells about the hour hand? _____

 Write two other questions that can be answered by looking at the title page and the table of contents.

When you give directions to make or do something, tell the steps in order. Think of something you know how to do or make. Use an idea from the box or your own. Write the steps in order.

- How to Make a Sandwich
- How to Wash Dishes
- How to Make a Bed
- How to Wash a Car

How to

Steps

Share your writing plan in class. Add ideas to the plan. Then use your plan to write a how-to paragraph. Include words like first, next, then, and last to show the order of steps. Put the writing in your folder.

Words can be grouped together in many ways. Write the words from "Old Ways of Telling Time" under the headings. Then write the word that matches each meaning.

<table>
<tr><td>candle</td><td>hourglass</td><td>sundial</td></tr>
<tr><td>clock</td><td>measured</td><td>sunrise</td></tr>
<tr><td>hour</td><td>minute</td><td>sunset</td></tr>
</table>

Things That Can Measure Time

_____

_____

Times of Day   **Parts of Time**

_____

_____

1. a clock that uses sand to tell time _____

2. found the size or amount of something _____

3. a stick of wax with string in the middle _____

4. the time when the sun comes up _____

5. a part of the day _____

6. a clock that uses shadows to tell time _____

 With a classmate, explain how you could use a candle to tell time.

Name _____

Think about the clocks in "Old Ways of Telling Time." Read each question and check (✓) the answer. Then tell why and give the page number for the answer.

1. If you lived in a rainy place, what kind of clock would be most useful?

   _____ a shadow stick

   _____ a sundial

   _____ a candle clock

   Why? _____ page _____

2. Which two clocks are alike?

   _____ an hourglass and a rope clock

   _____ a sundial and a shadow stick

   _____ a water clock and a sundial

   Why? _____ page _____

3. Which clock can be used again and again?

   _____ candle clock

   _____ rope clock

   _____ hourglass

   Why? _____ page _____

 If you did not want to keep making a new clock, would you make a candle or a water clock? Why?

"Old Ways of Telling Time" and "Tick Tock Clock," pages 203–209
Selection Comprehension: topic/main idea/details

Read these riddles. Circle the answers.

1. You check me to tell the time.
   I have a face.
   What am I?

   block
   clock
   quick

2. I am a messy kind of weather.
   You need to wear boots when
   I'm around. What am I?

   shiny
   shout
   slush

3. You use me to cover rips and
   tears. I am made of cloth.
   What am I?

   fetch
   scratch
   patch

4. You might see me in a bird cage.
   A parrot could sit on me and use
   me to swing. What am I?

   perch
   march
   birch

5. You can tie a rope and make me.
   You can join two pieces of rope
   with me. What am I?

   knot
   knock
   knee

6. You can use me to sew on a
   button. I belong on a finger.
   What am I?

   thanks
   thimble
   thief

7. I am very helpful when you rake
   leaves. You can dump them in me
   and carry them away. What am I?

   whisker
   whittle
   wheelbarrow

 Write riddles for the words that were not answers.

© D.C. Heath and Company

"Old Ways of Telling Time" and "Tick Tock Clock," pages 203–209
Decoding: consonant digraphs ch, ck, kn, sh, tch, th, wh

Name _____

Endings change word meanings. Read the sentence and the root word. Add es or ed to the word. Remember to change y to i or f to v first. Write the new word in the sentence. Read the sentence again to check your word.

worry   1. Long ago, people were not

_____ about time.

leaf   2. People told time by the falling

_____ and snow.

carry   3. The town crier _____ the news and told the time.

try   4. Later, people _____ to find better ways to tell time.

life   5. Today, our _____ are very busy.

hurry   6. Everyone _____ to get things done.

family   7. Some _____ have two or three clocks.

shelf   8. Homes have clocks on walls and _____.

city   9. In _____, the buildings have clocks.

fly   10. People say that time _____.

 Write the root words ending in y. Change the meaning by adding the ending (es or ed) that you did not use in the sentence.

© D.C. Heath and Company

"Old Ways of Telling Time" and "Tick Tock Clock," pages 203–209
Decoding: spelling changes (f to v, y to i before ending)

Name _____

Sometimes a writer gives clues to help you figure out what is not in the story. Read each story. Use the story clues to choose the sentence ending. Circle the letter.

1. Mr. Hawkins walked the horse out to the far field. All the lettuce had been picked, and it was time to plant the corn. But first Mr. Hawkins had to get the ground ready. So he hitched up the horse.
   Mr. Hawkins is going to _____ .
   a. take the children on horse rides
   b. plow the field

2. Little Sister jumped off the sidewalk and stamped her feet. Her shoes were soaked. "Oh, no!" said Mother. "Those shoes are brand new!"
   Little Sister is _____ .
   a. playing in a puddle
   b. making mud cakes

3. Sal had a water clock. One day, he noticed water pouring out of the pot. Sure enough, it had a hole in it. No wonder he couldn't tell the correct time. Sal got his toolbox.
   Sal is going to _____ .
   a. take a bath
   b. fix his water clock

 Circle the story words that are clues to the answers.

Name _____

Read the questions about the Index.
Check (✓) the answers.

> ### Index
> clockmakers, **39–43**
> clocks, **9–16**
> hourglasses, **12–13**
> sundials, **11–12**
> watches, **17–19, 21–29**

1. Why do you use an index?

   _____ to find the names of the chapters

   _____ to find the page numbers for subjects in a book

2. On what pages can you read about sundials?

   _____ 12–13

   _____ 11–12

3. What can you read about on page **40**?

   _____ hourglasses

   _____ clockmakers

4. What topic would tell the parts of a clock?

   _____ clockmakers

   _____ clocks

 Add sports watch and grandfather clock
to the Index.

"Old Ways of Telling Time" and "Tick Tock Clock," pages 203–209
Study Skills: parts of a book (index)

Name _____

**Read this story. Write the words from
"Dinosaur Facts" in the sentences. Read the
story again to check your words.**

brain   imagine   millions   walnut
footprints   jungles   peek

Dinosaurs roamed Earth _____ of years ago,
so you will never see a live one. You can only

_____ what it would be like to meet a dinosaur.

Dinosaurs walked through warm, thick _____ .
    Some dinosaurs, like Brachiosaurus, were huge. Others,
like Stegosaurus, were much smaller. Can you believe

Stegosaurus had a _____ as small as a

_____ ? So if you ever see any _____ ,

be careful! You might get a _____ at a dinosaur!

 Draw a picture of a dinosaur. Write two sentences about
it. Use some words from this page in your sentences.

Think about the dinosaurs you read about in "Dinosaur Facts." Write facts about the dinosaurs in the chart. Use your book to help you.

Dinosaurs—Terrible Lizards

I. Clues About Dinosaurs

   A. bones

   B. _____

II. Kinds of Dinosaurs

   A. Brachiosaurus

      1. plant eater

      2. _____

   B. _____

      1. _____

      2. row of pointed plates

   C. _____

      1. _____

      2. _____

   D. Tyrannosaurus

      1. _____

      2. _____

 What other facts can you write about dinosaurs? Add your facts to this chart.

"Dinosaur Facts," pages 212–219
Selection Comprehension: topic/main idea/details

Name _____

Endings change word meanings. Read the sentence and the root word. Add _er_ or _est_ to the word. Remember to change the root word ending in some words. Write the new word in the sentence. Read the sentence to check your word.

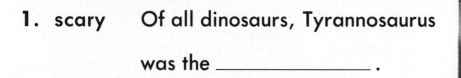

1. scary   Of all dinosaurs, Tyrannosaurus

was the _____ .

2. big   One of the _____ dinosaurs was the Brachiosaurus.

3. tall   It was _____ than a three-story building.

4. large   Not all of the dinosaurs were _____ than animals today.

5. tiny   One of the _____ dinosaurs was the size of a sparrow.

6. nice   But it was not the _____ because it ate its own kind.

7. light   The Stegosaurus was _____ in weight than a hippopotamus.

8. smart   And the hippopotamus is probably _____ .

 Look at the picture of the boy and the dinosaur. How much taller is the dinosaur?

Knowing how to divide words into syllables will help you read them. Write each word in syllables under the heading that shows how to divide the word.

around	cradle	snowsuit
asleep	flutter	spyglass
become	monkey	thimble
beehive	nearby	window
behave	puzzle	
channel	riddle	

Word parts <u>a</u>, <u>be</u>

_____

_____

_____

_____

Compound Words

_____

_____

_____

_____

Words ending in <u>le</u>

_____

_____

_____

Words with <u>VC/CV</u>

_____

_____

_____

 Add your own words to each list. Divide the words into syllables.

"Dinosaur Facts," pages 212–219
Decoding: syllable patterns VC/CV, Cle, compound words, word parts <u>a-</u>, <u>be-</u>

Synonyms are words that have the same or almost the same meaning. Read each sentence. Circle the word that is a synonym for the word in bold print.

world   1. In the days of dinosaurs, the planet was full of jungles.

wonder   2. Can you imagine what it would be like to follow a dinosaur through a jungle?

footprints   3. How large would its tracks be?

placed   4. What would it sound like when it raised its huge feet and set them down again?

believe   5. I think it would sound like the roll of a drum.

marched   6. Would its feet shake the ground as it walked through the forest?

scared   7. Would I be afraid?

crawl   8. I would probably creep under a giant plant and hide myself.

watchful   9. I would be careful not to move so the dinosaur wouldn't spot me.

learn   10. But just think how much I could discover about a dinosaur by watching one.

 Find synonyms on this page for **terrible lizard, woods, huge,** and **lifted.**

Name _____

Read these new facts about dinosaurs. Think about the important ideas. Write the facts.

Scientists have found some interesting new facts about dinosaurs. People who study dinosaurs once thought that all dinosaurs were very slow. Now they know that some moved fast. Some could run 30 miles an hour. Scientists have learned that dinosaurs lived in big family groups. Parent dinosaurs built nests for their babies. They hid them from enemies and fed them. There is still a lot to learn, but someday we will know everything about dinosaurs.

Topic   What are these sentences about?

_____

Main Idea   What is the most important idea?

_____

_____

Details   How did dinosaurs move and live?

_____   _____

_____   _____

_____   _____

_____

 Write a title for this story at the top of the page.

Name _____

Read these words and meanings from "Dinosaurs at Home." Write each word beside its meaning.

bandage   paste   scissors
corner   pencil
crayons   pieces

1. sticks of colored wax used to color _____

2. parts of something _____

3. glue _____

4. the point where two lines, sides, or walls meet _____

5. a strip of cloth used for any part of the body

   that has been hurt _____

6. a tool with two blades used for cutting _____

7. a tool used to write or draw _____

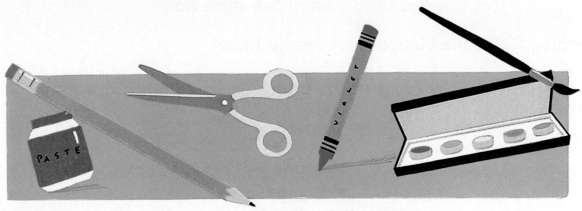

 List the words at the top under the following headings: Things That Are Sticky, Things That Mark, Tool for Cutting, Other.

Name _____

You read how to make a dinosaur in "Dinosaurs at Home." Read these sentences. Check (✓) the one that tells what you do before the numbered sentence.

1. Fold the dinosaur in half.

   _____ Fold the dinosaur along its back.

   _____ Trace the dinosaur on paper.

2. Color your dinosaur.

   _____ Paste both sides of the dinosaur's head together.

   _____ Cut out the dinosaur.

3. Tape a piece of straw on the inside of each foot.

   _____ Color the sky.

   _____ Cut the straw into four pieces.

4. Color the sky, sun, grass, flowers, and mountains.

   _____ Cut out one long side of the shoe box.

   _____ Put the bandage on really tight.

5. Press the sticky parts of the bandage firmly onto the stone.

   _____ Put the tree in the corner.

   _____ Use the bandage to make little twigs stick to the back of the biggest stone.

 Draw a picture that shows how the earth looked when dinosaurs were alive. Add a title.

"Dinosaurs at Home," pages 220–225
Selection Comprehension: sequence

Name _____

Endings change word meanings. Read the sentences and the root words. Add <u>ly</u> or <u>ful</u> to make a new word. Remember to change <u>y</u> to <u>i</u> in some words. Write the new word in the sentence. Read the sentence again to check your word.

slow   **1.** The dinosaur walked _____ through the city streets.

color   **2.** Its _____ body towered over the buildings.

wild   **3.** It moved its head _____ .

noisy   **4.** The monster growled _____ .

hungry   **5.** It stared _____ down at the empty sidewalks.

play   **6.** This was not a _____ dinosaur.

fear   **7.** The _____ people hid in the doorways.

quick   **8.** Hundreds of police _____ blocked off the streets.

hope   **9.** Now everyone was _____ .

thank   **10.** I was _____ this was only a movie.

 Write other root words. Add <u>ly</u> or <u>ful</u>. Write the new words in a sentence. Use your book for help.

Read these ideas about dinosaurs. Then read the sentences that tell what happened. Write why.

Why did all the dinosaurs die? Some scientists think that a long time ago Earth and a tiny planet bumped into each other. Because of the crash, a lot of dust was thrown up into the air. The dust was so thick that it blocked any sunlight from reaching the ground. Because they had no sunlight, most of the plants died. The dinosaurs that fed on plants had no food and died. The dinosaurs that fed on other dinosaurs had nothing to eat, and they died too.

1. A lot of dust was thrown up into the air. Why? _____

_____

2. The sunlight did not reach the ground. Why? _____

_____

3. The plants died. Why? _____

4. Plant-eating dinosaurs died. Why? _____

_____

5. Then meat-eating dinosaurs died. Why? _____

_____

 Choose a fact that tells what happened. Ask a classmate to tell why.

"Dinosaurs at Home," pages 220–225
Comprehension: cause-effect

© D.C. Heath and Company

Sometimes when you read a story, you have to look for clues to answer questions. Read the story and the questions. Fill in the circle.

Brachiosaurus stood next to a lake. A herd of Stegosaurs had just eaten all the bottom leaves of a giant plant. Brachiosaurus stretched its long neck and ate the leaves at the top of the plant.

Suddenly, Brachiosaurus heard the hungry roar of Tyrannosaurus. To get away, Brachiosaurus walked into the deepest part of the lake. Tyrannosaurus looked angrily at Brachiosaurus's head in the middle of the lake.

1. Why did the Stegosaurs eat the bottom leaves?
   ○ They were afraid of Brachiosaurus.
   ○ They could reach only the bottom leaves.

2. Why did Brachiosaurus walk into the lake?
   ○ It wanted to get away from Tyrannosaurus.
   ○ It wanted some water.

3. Why was Tyrannosaurus angry?
   ○ It wanted Brachiosaurus to throw down some leaves.
   ○ It wanted to eat Brachiosaurus.

4. Why didn't Tyrannosaurus follow Brachiosaurus into the lake?
   ○ It was too deep.
   ○ The water was too cold.

 Underline the story clues that helped you answer the questions.

Name _____

In this story about Nessie, the writer did not give details that tell why things happened. Choose details from the box or add your own to the story. Write all the sentences in order.

- Something that looks like a dinosaur has been seen in Scotland.
- It lives in Loch Ness in Scotland.
- The pictures are fuzzy.
- The water in the lake is muddy.

A dinosaur may still be alive today! It is called Nessie. Photographs have been taken of Nessie. Some people who have seen the pictures do not believe it is a dinosaur. No one has been able to find Nessie under the water.

_____

_____

_____

_____

Read your story in class. Then look at the writing in your folder. Add details to your writing to tell why things happened. Write all the sentences in order. Then put the writing in your folder.

"Dinosaurs at Home," pages 220–225
Language: writing process (revising)